Born to Love, Cursed to Feel

Revised Edition

Also by Samantha King Holmes

Born to Love, Cursed to Feel
Don't Tell Me Not to Ask Why
We Hope This Reaches You in Time
She Fits Inside These Words

Born to Love, Cursed to Feel.

Revised Edition

Samantha King Holmes

This one's for me & anyone who needs it.

Perfect

You're a beautiful kind of madness
A misunderstood truth

O, the things they could learn
from the darkness that is hidden
behind your eyes

So gifted, yet your talents are wasted
You gave up chasing dreams
Reality hit, and you got a taste of failure

Cautious now about bearing your soul
For if others saw you fully exposed
they may not love you like they claim to

Time and experience have taught you to trust no one
Friends, lovers, and even family have forsaken you
You keep the shattered pieces of your heart in a box
Stitching, gluing, and staying up all night
trying to put it back together

Attempting to fill the void that was left
Moving from one man to the next
It seems no one can satisfy the appetite
for affection that you seek

Continually picking at old wounds
they never heal properly
You have no real home
too restless to stay in one place

You are reckless, selfish, stubborn
sometimes rude
You've bottled up the pain
of so much that has been done

When you're hurt
You close into yourself, shut down
You love attention, and yet
love being by yourself more
May God have mercy on your soul
For you are truly lost

Daily, you fight your demons
Yet no one knows of that which you endure
You bear it alone, never speaking of it

You can blame the broken home
from which you came
Or the environment that you grew up in
The people who tore you down so young
You can point the finger
at those who have whispered behind your back
They all have played a role in your development
But looking so deep into the past
will keep you from moving forward

You must love yourself more
than these people claim they do
Look at where you stand now
No one can know the things
you have endured like you

You've never claimed to be perfect
Your flaws tell your story
There is no need to hide them

Eyes Open

The scary part
is I knew exactly
how bad you were for me
and yet that didn't stop me
from loving you

One

I don't look for you in anything
For in everything, you are
Where I am, you exist
In each breath, every smile
and even in moments of pain

I am cloaked in your spirit
utterly submerged in you
Reality so beautiful
something I can see and feel
You're someone I believe in

How was I so fortunate to come across such bliss?
Kissed by Heaven's favor, perhaps
Spoke it into existence, maybe
You and I were always made for this moment
Fate may have brought us together
but we chose to stay

Unyielding

It's been years, and your life still has no room for me
I write myself in where I can

A Broken Cycle

I feel sometimes that I punish myself
Allow myself to be overrun by men
who can't match the passion I exert
Teaching you how to give more, love harder
is simply getting exhausting
And the disappointments have hardened my heart

I think you enjoy my misery
and maybe I've become a glutton for pain

Good-bye

I thought I would be devastated without you
I was waiting for everything to rip apart
The sky didn't come crashing down
Air still flows through my lungs
Blood surges through my veins

I thought I would lie down in surrender
I didn't give my heart enough credit
I sit here waiting for it
The realization that you are
a part of my Life no more

I've wrapped my mind around the notion
It's possible I already cried enough
Perhaps the year and a half spent
trying to make sense of all this
has finally drained me

Maybe, just maybe, I always knew I deserved better
but was too afraid to accept it
I feel as if I should mourn us
Except I sit here relieved
I gave you my all
and took the loss that even that wasn't enough

Maybe, just maybe, you were never meant to be mine,
no matter how hard I loved you
You broke me in ways that I've never experienced before
and if I'm wise enough
will not allow myself to endure again

I no longer think of you as often
or long for you at night
There are moments when you are missed
that I cast into the light of your negligence
and allow to burn away and die

I hungered for Love, your Love, and starved
No worries; I carry no hate in my heart for you
I want no parts of you to linger long here
You weren't ready for the Love I could give
Now I have a different plan in mind

Defeat

I've withered in your shadow
My love no longer grows in leaps and bounds
It is not rooted
There is no nourishment to soak in
I am left ravenous for your attention

Some kind of passion, a simple touch
The air between the sweet words that are whispered
None of it is given, and yet I crave so much
You know it

You stopped adoring me the way you used to
My mind has registered this
My heart just won't accept it
It believes that if I keep trying
one day we'll make it
Somewhere, deep down, though
I know this isn't true

In time, you will simply be diminished
to the man who broke me to the point
that I was forced to face myself
Forever, you will live between
the black and white of these pages

I am somehow more of myself now
This has been no mild transition
My back was broken to please you
My mind strained
My heart tested, and it persevered
in ways unknown to it before

There is no satisfaction in this stunted growth
I've imprisoned myself to doing my best to love
a man who can't love me back the way I need him to
The way I deserve
You've always had the knowledge of my dreams
You just decided not to be a part of them

Wrong Mark

Do you ever think of me in a prolonged agony?
Does your soul search for me while you rest?
Have you forgotten my eyes or the fire they set ablaze
when you gazed into them?
I miss you
I sit here lost, genuinely yearning to know what
you're doing and where you are
O, sweet Cupid, what have you done?
I call foul play here
How is it I came to love a man
who now feels like a stranger?

Vow of Silence

I spoke out of fear, and you ignored me
I spoke out of pain, and you didn't listen
I spoke out of love, and you walked away
So now I speak of nothing

Karma

She's been watching me
She's been patient
Lying dormant in anticipation
She's waited for this moment
I feel her breath on my neck

Forgiven but not forgotten
My time must be paid in full
Suffering has not yet ended
It has only pooled,
waiting to drown me in my shame

It knows all, despite the trails that have been covered
The countless names of offenses
that never made it to the ear of their victim
I have not always been good
but he has made me want to be more

The depths of love I feel for him cannot be uttered
So rare that I tread softly
In fear that if I approach too fast it will flee

She knows this
I've caught her lurking around the corners of my joy
The weight of her presence unhinging my sanity
She's a sign that a storm is inevitable
I'm down on my knees, begging
"Please don't do this to me"
No form of redemption is enough

A simple explanation that
I was young and dumb will not save me
I'm starting to wonder if my paranoia
is punishment enough
Yet I know better
My debt must be paid in full
Karma, release me

Woke

I get it, doing what you can
to not think about the girl you can't have
The one who told you her fears
like you were going to be the last one to hear it

She only gives herself in pieces
Rare and very few have her
in her uninhibited form
With you, words came easily
but were never really needed

Sometimes you lie awake at night
hoping that she will call and say she misses you
It doesn't happen
She never really quite said the right thing
Something always held her back
It was written on her face

There's no relief to what you feel
For as much as she is your reality
she plagues your dreams as well
So, eyes open, you conjure thoughts of her
allow fantasies to create what reality won't
Eyes closed, she's right there
but no matter how much you reach for her
there is no feeling of her face against your hand

You can't say you Love her yet
One day, though, you would like to find that you do
To feel her touch, her warmth
her relentless need for you
A dream unattainable
You wake up from it, every time she says his name
A sober realization that she is owned by no one
and yet chained to a man you've only ever heard of

What does he do for her?
Is it him she dreams of?
Does he crave her the way you do?
Would he understand the persistent desire
to be there when she needs it?

She cried today; today you saw her cry
You watched the tears roll down her face
as the mask of her strength melted before you
You wanted to stay
but had already begun to say good-bye
She grasped your hand, tried to anchor you to the lie
but you had already seen the truth

No matter how good you were
or how much you desired her
she would be his till she decided otherwise
Caring for someone who loves another
is no easy task
You found the courage to walk away
and not look back
Those tears may follow you for some time
but like her will become a distant memory

Life is about the choices we make
the moments we don't see coming
and the strength to do what's best for ourselves
despite how much it may hurt
You were brave enough to wake up
now don't go back to sleep

Sweet Deception

It all seemed so perfect
I guess lies are that way
They wait until you're entangled in them
Wrapped in their beauty
The minute you start to believe they're real
they rip apart all the hope you had left

Anguish

I went to the dark part of my mind
Put one foot on the shovel and dug you up
I needed to look one more time
just one more glance
My mistake was thinking it was really over
Once free, you decided to wreak havoc
on the rest of my mind
Making it dark too

Vital

I want to be singed by your passion
Release me from this existence
and reincarnate me into the air you breathe
Let me be what sustains you
Leaving a trace of my imprint
pumping through your veins

Home

His dirty socks and shoes on the floor
My hair clogging up the drain
Clothes scattered everywhere
And the loud tapping of the typewriter
I got him for his birthday
I was once alone
then this chaos ensued
that we now call a home
Despite whatever complaints I may have
I wouldn't want it any other way
or with anyone else

Partner in Crime

Friend, let my eyes be the guide to your beauty
that you have yet to discover

Let my heart be your safe haven
when your world begins to darken
and storms wash away the essence of your faith

Let my fingers entwine with yours
serving as reassurance that there is nothing
that you will ever have to face alone

Ghosts of New York

I would like to think
that they all have their own stories
But we never ask
we don't even know their names
Or what has brought them to their knees
and humbled them enough
to lie on the floor of a station
Or sit on a train all night long
just to have somewhere warm to sleep
They are gawked at
People will leave their presence
to avoid the smell
but they have nowhere to wash their bodies

On those days when you've argued
with your boss or a friend
something didn't go your way
and you think you have it bad
they are walking, breathing, living evidence
that someone out there truly has it worse

We've made ourselves so cold, so immune
that we've taken the humanity out
of what's happening in front of us
So, yes, I would like to believe that
when I give them that dollar
they aren't going to use it
to put a needle in their arm
And if they should, who am I to judge?
Maybe when you're already that low
all there is left to live for is chasing that high

Life's Student

There is growth in pain
You just have to find the lesson and learn it

Thinking Out Loud

So self-destructive
I'm waiting for the implosion
For the Universe's infinite wisdom
to cave in my chest and abolish all my fears
To be driven so deep into the possibilities
that I am blinded by the light
Forced to once again dream genuinely
Before the days of naysayers and doubts

I'm in the stairwell hiding from the people
hiding from the noise
Can they see my insecurities as vividly as I do?
Do they possess that kind of vision?
Or are they so lost in their own self-turmoil
that they don't even notice I'm depleted?
A remnant of a dreamer gone mad
A hopeless romantic who hasn't been fed
An artist starving for Life, to Live

Justice

Living, but not really living
Breathing, but not really savoring
every precious breath
Believing, but at the same time doubting
that this pain will ever cease to exist
Overwhelming doses of emotion
Can someone prescribe me something
so I can go numb?
I need a moment
Something more than these
unrelenting episodes of sorrow and anguish
Is there no joy left for me?
Will there ever be a moment
when I can truly smile?
Will there ever be a time
when I won't attempt to imagine your face?
I'd give anything to have a second chance
To give you a second thought
I'm engulfed in what could have been
Consumed in it so much
That the present all seems like a blur
I've done many things
that I will choose to forget
But this is by far my worst regret
I cannot change what has been done
No matter how many stars I wish upon

So I'll go on
Smiling, but not really smiling
Loving, but not really loving
Living, but not really living

Comfort

When I hit that wall
and I am going to hit it
as I'm lying on the floor
consumed by despair
don't try and pick me up
Don't whisper words of comfort
Don't tell me it's going to be ok
Let me be in this moment
when I think it's not
Lie beside me, and let me find hope
in the comfort of your presence
Let me deal with my thoughts and fears
I will eventually reprimand myself for indulging
in such an emotion for so long
I will want to get up and keep moving forward
Until then, let me lie here, and let the salt of my tears
sting the wounds you can't see
Until I'm ready, let me be
I have to heal myself

Fool Me Twice

I took a risk by reinvesting myself
I took an even bigger one
when I began to care
But I tightened the knot of the noose
around my neck
when I began to Love you again
You kicked the chair out from under me
so I didn't even have to jump

Canvas

Forlorn, lost
I thought I would have it by now
I'm somewhere between
"Is this really my life?" and
"Where am I right now?"
I measured whom I was supposed to be
against the picture that you painted
Now I'm stuck with this brush
my chaotic thoughts and this canvas
I never wanted perfect; I just wanted happy
I'm still figuring out what that looks like

Moving On

Your nighttime fool
Your daytime Lover
I should have been off this road
about four text messages and three missed calls ago
Sitting in the dark, pondering the thought of you
Dear Sandman, why have you yet to come?
I need this slumber
The pain has finally overrun me
So low, I think the ground
has become envious of my position
If you no longer desired my Love
then you simply could have told me
There was no need to drag me along
and punish me this way
My friends are exhausted
from the relentless phone calls of sobs and silence
the "help me" look that has invaded my face
and the absence of who I was before us
This isn't some timeless romance, just a tragedy
I'm done letting you have that kind of control
I'm no longer waiting for the ending
I'm writing one without you

Old School

Don't you miss the days when being in a relationship
meant there was no competition?
When separation was a last resort
after all other means had been exhausted
When you didn't wait up all night
creeping through social media
to know what your partner was doing
Love letters were handwritten and saved
They knew your favorite candy
And laughter was in abundance
Are we all so focused on not getting hurt
that we'd destroy another to spare ourselves?
Do you remember when "I love you"
meant something? Did those days ever exist?

Other Woman

It's 3 a.m.
My phone's going off
He's on his way
I should be sleeping
rather than waiting anxiously for him
It can't be helped, though
He's my addiction

A self-inflicted agony
I let him in
He never stays long
regardless of how much I plead with him to
He already has a home where he belongs
I was just a refuge
for what he wouldn't share with her

This week, she and I finally met
She caught me staring in his direction
I was in shock
The knowledge of her
was always in my possession
but I acted as if she were nonexistent
somewhat irrelevant to my life

To cover up for the intrusion my eyes made
he introduced me as an old friend
I went along with the story
She believed him

My eyes scanned her curvy frame
They stopped at her protruding stomach
She noticed, then gushed that she was five months
"It's a boy"
No wonder she was glowing
She was truly beautiful

I felt the bile rise in the back of my throat
She insisted that she get my information
so when the baby shower was held I could come
If she only knew that my info had been across his lips
and held within his hands

After we departed, he texted
"That was a close one. Good job, though, babe.
See you later on."
I cried the tears that because of her ignorance
she would never shed
To go on like this
would truly be the cause of my demise

At midnight, he texted me
At 1 a.m., he called
At 2 a.m., he wrote again
At 3 a.m., I turned off

Role Reversal

Let's trade places
You wait up all night
for a phone call that never comes
You can fall asleep
to the empty nothingness instead of my voice
You can feel like you're giving
your all for nothing and wake up alone

No text, no call, no indication
that you were thought of
No apology, just empty promises
Words of sentiment that lack the real affection
Try feeling like you're compromising yourself
once again to receive nothing in return

You can open up your heart
and have nothing fill it
Wonder every morning
why you're even doing this
and then shed the tears I'll never see
You can watch me walk away
But there is no need to switch sides
to see that happen

My Truth

I lost everything trying to do right
My sanity, my hope
and eventually the will to keep trying
What was shameful wasn't the way you loved me
but the way I loved you
You could never match what I gave
and deep down I always knew it

Tomorrow

How I allowed myself to get here
is still a question I have yet to answer
The walls cry out his name
The shirt that he left behind
that I am now wearing
is drenched in his scent
His side of the bed is unbearably vacant
Everything reminds me of him
It's as if I'm being punished
I should leave
Yet I sit and wait
for a man I can't call my own
A man who says he sees us together in the future
but can't commit to me today
It's been over a year now
I've come to realize
I deserve better
Giving in, succumbing to his needs and desires
is a full-time job all its own
For which I put in overtime, and yet I go unpaid
I allowed myself to be enslaved
by my so-called feelings
For a man unworthy of my time and effort
One day, I'm going to walk away and not look back
At least that's what I keep telling myself
My phone rings; it's him

He's coming over
I want to fuss
Tell him it's either something more or he can leave
but somehow his smile soothes me
Once in his grasp,
his touch feeds my need for affection
I fall asleep in his arms
thinking maybe I'll have the strength to leave
Tomorrow

A Stolen Lesson

You stole my voice
How could I let you?
Silencing my own thoughts and dreams
Because they were so loud, they drowned you out

You stole my time
How could I give it so easily?
Hours were toiled over what you were doing
whether or not you really loved me
Minutes were spent in your presence
while it was only for seconds
that I was actually happy

You stole my pride
I became a fool, your own personal jester
For I would rather see you smile
than taste the bitterness of my tears
when I was without you

You stole my love
Why me? Why you? Why now?
I didn't know I was giving it
Until it was already gone
Even when my mind was screaming
"You know better"

I may have suffered but in the end have won
For you had to take all these things
and now are left with nothing
While I have learned my lesson

Behind Brown Eyes

It'd be ignorant of me
To try and sit here and discuss your pain
Pretend I have the solution
As if this were a simple problem
and not the destruction of your heart once again
I'm sending my regards
I simply can't bear to watch you fade into your grief
Stiff, cold, too far away for me to reach
I want to see the joy that was once in your eyes
The thirst for adventure
That hunger for life
I don't know if I ever told you
that you made me better
And although I don't say much
I've always been around
just in case you need me
Pain is inevitable
It's how you choose to heal that matters
I apologize that the desecration of your
bountiful optimism was so swift
Laid out for others to see
Don't give him the satisfaction
of dwelling on words of sentiment
Those were clearly lies
Actions will always trump pretty words
I won't offend you by

simply stating that in time you'll heal
My friend, all I will say is that I love you
And until the shards of your heart
are stitched back together, fully revived
I have no problem with letting you borrow mine

Relapse

Lying in her bed, she thought it was over
The cold sweats had stopped months ago
She hadn't craved it for weeks
With each passing day
the hours no longer seemed so endless
Just when she thought she had broken free
she was sinking under again
At first, there was no desire to stray
No yearning for the familiar gratification
of rising so high above the burdens
that the world heaved onto her shoulders
That beautiful paradise, that intoxicating escape
She got a taste of that oh-so-compelling sensation
and didn't realize she was under
until he was penetrating all of her forces
It was an all-too-familiar scene
Remembering the crash is hard
when you're knee-deep in the haze of ecstasy
She awoke alone
to the feeling of defeat
It wasn't worth it
It never was

9–5

Time ticks away
Screaming its objection
That the hours should pass so leisurely
Till I should be with you again
It is only the passing of such that could tear us apart
Good or bad, whatever the day should bring
I will never mind
As long as you are always the conclusion

Dear . . .

You're the poem I couldn't finish
The journey I should have never started
I saw tragedy in our ending
My pen bled its heart out trying to change it
You were the fight I didn't want to lose
The addiction I didn't want to quit
Yet there was only one of us holding on
I wasn't attached to the man you are
But the one you could be
I tried to build where there was no foundation
Create a fairy tale on blank pages
But some stories need not be told, let alone written
You'll read my words and won't be moved
Your arrogance will not soften
You won't be changed
Your heart, if you should have one
will not bend or break
The worst part of it all
is this poem is about you
and you'll never even know it

Breaking Point

"I'm sorry" is no longer a healing balm
"It won't happen again" is just another lie
I see the remorse on your face
I can just no longer sympathize
You've drained me of whatever ability
I had left to dig a little deeper and
believe this was worth saving
I won't be staying tonight
I won't be coming back tomorrow
You can keep your watered-down
promises of forever

Insanity

If I'm losing my mind
it's because I've allowed myself to believe
I can stand tall in something that's sinking
without going under

Confession

"I hate you" wouldn't quite do it
"I forgive you" isn't quite my speed
"I regret meeting you" would be a lie
The best thing for me
was removing you from my life
That, I am sure of

Solitary

I can't stop; I won't
When I do
loneliness creeps in
The burning flames of sadness
lick against my skin
My heart is engulfed in the sensation
that despite it all
I'm alone

In the Lonely Hour

We yearn so badly to be healed
We let anyone in
We cram them into what small space we have left
Hoping they have good intentions

Fin

I feel sick
Completely exposed, vulnerable
I have never shown a truer form of myself
than when in your arms
It is displayed on my face
In the increasing beat of my heart
My mind abhors you
For she has yet to find peace since you arrived
My eyes simply shun the sight of you
It sends me down a relentless spiral of flashbacks
Can you see that the memories that once brought me joy
now cause utter pain?
Do you torture me on purpose?
I have never hated or loved you more
It is not that I regret
what we once meant to each other
It's just that the days that I no longer reminisce
over us couldn't come sooner

December

People always ask
"When did you know?"
It could have been when I woke up
and watched you rest peacefully beside me
Or all those times I learned how much we're alike
But it was when we had that fight
I wanted to cry and laugh hysterically
We didn't leave
We sat in silence
The reason behind it all so small
I knew then just how much I loved you
And as you crossed over and merely
wrapped me in your arms
I knew just how much you loved me

Double-Edged Sword

I can't get back the hours, the effort
or that little piece of me that believed in you
You would think I'm the one who suffered here
but that's only cause you haven't figured out
what you lost

Gone

Every move you made
you were allowed to
I saw it coming
I didn't move out of the way of disaster
I stood in it
Taking in the chaos around me
I refused to bend
The pain was internal
But I had to withstand this, you
You couldn't say good-bye
So, I collected my things and moved on without you

His Sorrow

The notes on his heart never manifest to be heard
The dreams that were once his love for life
now rest soundly with his fears
Nothing tastes as sweet
The colors have lost their radiance
Life seems like it's dwindling away
Just grains of sand lost in an hourglass
The hours of contemplation
and strain perceptible on his face
Hair disheveled, thoughts scattered
To savor this mild existence is now meaningless
There are no tears shed
for the broken pieces of a man's heart
Good guys finish last too frequently
They both said "I love you"
He was the only one who meant it

Unforgiven

I've tried to think of the words to tell you
Create a masterpiece of my pain
Paint it against the walls of your mind
So you can't forget
what your negligence has manifested
I strove for perfection
A compilation of words
that could invoke the emotion
My heart bleeds
when the sound of your voice reaches my ears
The conflict between it and my mind
For I am old enough to know
But young enough not to care that
I knew you were no good for me
I wanted to make your blue sky gray
Let the clouds shower upon you
The tears shed over the moments when I realized
that you never cared as much as I did
What I desired, what I yearned for you to see
can simply be understood by me saying
You broke the best part of me
And, no, you're not forgiven

Solace

I consistently neglect you
Attempt to replace you with others
Yet you always allow me to return
The yearning in the bottom of my stomach
The notion that something is missing
can be filled with no one but you
I try to deny it, but you give me purpose
Without you, I'm nothing
No cliché intended; I mean it
When my face is stained with tears
you are there to console me
When my heart is filled with joy
you are there to relish it
You know of all my secrets and fears
All the while you have never judged me
You'll let me pour out my heart
in the early hours of the morning
You never complain of my repetitive mistakes
but serve as a witness to all the ways
I've learned not to find Love
My Confidant, My Best Friend
the Essence of my Soul
Poetry, you are now and will always be
the better part of me

Retrospect

I blamed you so long for who I became
It was much easier than facing
that I allowed myself to become that

Quicksand

I wrote my last letter
Left it on the bed
Took it all in once more
Dropped my keys on the table
Unhinged what doubts were left
Then I walked away without looking back
A memory of how I got here
evoked with each step taken
The hours spent waiting up for you to get home
The countless mornings I awoke
to find myself still alone
The never-ending pleas of "Please just listen"
fell upon ears that weren't ready to hear it
Casual conversations led to arguments
of "Where have you been?" and "What are we?"
My hopes for "us" began to weigh me down
It seemed no matter what was done
all that was said
the harder I fought
the faster I began to sink
paralyzed, submerged in my fears
I went from blaming me to you to me again
to coming to terms with the fact
that just because you Love someone
doesn't mean you're supposed to be with them

Perception

I lost myself
Weighed down by the emotions
that chained me to your existence
I found when I unlocked
what bound me
that I felt different
A smile no longer seemed so painful
with you not around
The good moments could be enjoyed
even if not shared
Every second wasn't given to the thought of you
I realize now how much I was killing me loving you
You may not have noticed
the pain that your uncertainty caused
The walls your lies built up
The fabrications you told that made me hope
to only then shatter on the reality of who you are
I loved you with my heart
But I forgot to do it with my eyes open
Lesson learned

Untitled

I died a thousand deaths
Trying to get you to Love me once
You never did
There's a part of me that didn't survive "us"

Peace of Mind

It's impossible to write down
every emotion that has been stirred
Write an obituary
for every tear that has fallen
Meeting its end upon my face
To give a voice to all the thoughts
existing solely to taunt me
Screaming their position, debating their importance
Insisting, even pleading for a moment of focus
"Solve me before you move on to the next"
Silently waiting for action to be taken on their behalf
Hoping their simple existence isn't in vain
This isn't where I want to be
Nor do I know where I am going
Hopefully, I'll find my peace on the way

Try

Is there no humanity left?
Does there not reside in the hearts
of any one person some compassion?
I know you think ill of my actions
I just do not know how to proceed
To somehow pretend that everything is alright
when it isn't
The words no longer form so easily
around the thought of you
So nothing that escapes me comes out right
I sit silently awaiting my soul to awaken
For something entirely magnificent to happen
to make this fine
It hasn't; dare I say it ever will?
There is no comfort rooted
in the sound of your voice
I just can't quite figure out how to mend the bonds
that have become unhinged
Mask the hesitation
to once again walk alongside you
into whatever form of danger or happiness
that lurks along the road
I searched to find where it had all gone wrong
Leaving me to wonder, are we to just start again?
Don't hate me
You believe I'm not trying

but each day is a struggle
My forgiveness isn't going to be instantaneous
Your betrayal wasn't expected
Anything worth working at takes time
So if you choose to stay
have no expectations
from which to fall, disappointed
If you choose to go
I will respect your wishes
Just know that I did in fact try

Fraud

While you were claiming to protect me from others
someone should have protected me from you

Intimacy

I'd rather you fall in love with my naked soul
than my naked body
I am more than breasts and ass
I am a sensation
I am to be felt without being touched
I am to be understood without being seen

The Endless Struggle

I write what I can't say
I weep for these lost emotions
These voiceless, unclaimed soldiers
that go to battle every day
Only to lose their lives
spilling out onto my cheeks
So many casualties have been laid to rest
upon my pillowcase
What should bring my head solace
is now a graveyard for abandoned feelings
I sit up and work it over and over in my mind
Is there any logic to it all?
For that to truly exist, emotion would need to cease
I struggle with the war
that's continuing inside me as we speak
Defined by impulsions, confined

Inescapable Truth

Words escape me now
in the time that I need them most
What is there left to say
that hasn't already been said?
What path hasn't been laid before our feet to try?
Trapped within the ruins of what this once was
We're somewhere under the rubble
Your name has been spoken
from my lips a million times
You haven't noticed
You feel I don't listen
I'm just waiting for something profound to be said
to make the void stop growing
No longer your muse
My value in your eyes has depleted
You seek the benefit of a love worth having
I see the benefit of one worth keeping
When did we become so mean?
I'll type it out
and still won't be able to capture the sorrow felt
from watching in horror all that we are becoming

Long Distance

My fingers stroke a dirty screen
Aching to feel his skin beneath them
I lie next to it, pretending I'm really there beside him
We stare at each other
knowing we have other things to do
The energy so magnetic, we delay leaving
I'm living and breathing here
but my heart is so far away
I yearn to be in his embrace
To know he is safe and well
The fact that we dream under the same sky
should bring comfort
But a sunset is just not the same through a picture
Our moments are shared and stored
but my desire is to feel them completely
I would gladly weather any storm
if he were literally next to me
For how can I shun the wind and the rain
while I sit with my Blessing
They have their purpose in Life
and I believe his is to love me as I love him
For now until what I want comes to be
I'll appreciate that God thought fondly enough to have
our paths cross and be so intertwined
That I get to laugh, love, smile, and be weird
Even if, for now, it's through a screen

Love

Are you tired of me saying your name?
Are you ashamed that I declare you so often
when most times it seems that it was in vain?
Are you mad that I am not more cautious
when I play your card?
Or are you just tired of watching me
stuff my pockets with the broken pieces of my heart?

Remnants

There comes a point when there aren't any tears left
When we have lost what we've held dear
All that's left are the memories
They taunt us
Reminding us of the happiness that we once felt
Awakening the pain that isn't easily released
One day, when we've found closure
and the scar tissue covers the wounds left
The memories will no longer seem like punishment
but serve as evidence of our resilience

Gamble

We give people multiple chances
hoping that they'll change
I don't know if it speaks less of them
for taking advantage
or less of us for refusing
to accept who they are

The Beginning

The beauty of first dates and first kisses
Of "I miss you" and "No, you hang up first"
Of staring into each other's eyes
and then laughing for no reason
Trying hard not to admit that the tingling sensation
in your stomach wasn't just unexpected but exquisite

Secret

The name you'll whisper but won't say out loud
The call you'll make in the middle of the night
As you twist words around and around
draining them of their sweetness
All to lie in between sheets
I am the one you cry out for when you're alone
I hate you
You've made me a detested secret
I'm ashamed that I crawled into the closet
that you built for me
Believing I deserve no more than that
I've marked the days
that I allowed myself to be so stupid
It may take double that or more
for me to forgive myself
For you, I feel no grace or empathy
I felt for you with what I had
and you took the best of me
Sufficient enough to attain, be consumed in
Yet never good enough to be claimed
I hope when you open the door
to find that I'm no longer there
that for one second you sit where I sat
and contemplate whether you ever deserved
someone like me

Over

It became too much
The arguments became louder, the fights often
Trust diminished over time, and lines were crossed
Drunken phone calls and bad decisions
It wasn't from a lack of trying but a lack of respect
Bridges turned to ashes
No need to mourn them

Hindsight

I screamed; you didn't hear me
I walked away; you didn't chase
I've found that our value lies not in what's spoken
but in all the things your actions say
I've cried more than I've smiled
I've lost more than I've gained
I'm tired of sacrificing
but no big fuss
You won't even notice what's happened
until it's already too late

Progress

So often we are defined by what we've done
and the mistakes we've made
For once, I would like to be
measured by the steps I took today
rather than the footprints of yesterday

Haunted

I'd give anything to steal a glance of your happiness
Feel your fingers interlocked in mine
My love for you hasn't died or subsided
I tried to bury it deep somewhere
but it finds me
I'm living in a constant state of flashbacks
The past so vivid, leaking into my present
I can't get away from you
One minute you're here, the next minute
I can't even reach out to touch you
I know it's wrong to linger
for so long on this feeling
You're not coming back
Is my regret for not keeping you so strong
that your existence haunts me?

Last Leg

The power of words
Emotions that hang in the air
The space between what is said
and what hasn't quite made it to the surface
Time's significance lived out in stolen moments
Lost in the abyss of negligence
The climb seems more strenuous
Life has upped the ante; there's more at stake
We strive for a better understanding
yet rest on the platforms of our own ignorance
Too stubborn to truly admit
that there may be something to what is being said
A possibility that our own sides
aren't the only right path
The haze between our perceptions of what is
and what could be has grown as thick as the tension
Helplessly feeling around for some
common ground to hold on to
Afraid of what will happen should this bond crumble
We try to build bridges, but they break
So I watch from a distance
Again, admonished to be simply an admirer
There was once a time where we were truly happy

Sacrifice

The war between my mind and my heart
has been the biggest destruction of my peace
To think I turned the better parts of me
against one another
all for the sake of keeping you

Disorder

My room is a mess; my life is cluttered
I'm obsessed with love from an indifferent lover
I wait in anticipation for a revelation
that isn't coming
I don't know what I want more
unconditional love or just something
to stop the longing

Foolish

He was never really mine
and in truth he was never really hers either
The only thing he belonged to was his desires
and anyone who would fulfill them

Abandonment Issues

I always wondered
why it was so easy for people to leave
What I should have questioned was
why I wanted so badly for them to stay

Revelation

I've learned to face my demons
I'm just learning not everybody can handle them

False Hope

Stop waiting for it to make sense
Stop using that as an excuse to leave the door open
It's not closure that you're seeking
It's this hope that despite what's gone wrong
everything can go back to normal

Pause

I want to press stop
but can't seem to find the button
The words are stuck on replay in my mind
What's being said is loud and clear
It's what isn't that is resonating
We went too far; we should have stopped
Pain met me last night and left with me this morning
My mind is two seconds from imploding
"It's not that serious"
So why do I feel so slighted?
I prefer not to dwell on this
but the tears shed from our fight haunt me
The realization that their existence mattered not
is a weight I didn't plan to carry
I was wrong; you were wrong
Fingers can be pointed, but both our hands are filthy
Voices were raised to tune the other out
Points were spoken in vain
We could have stopped; we should have stopped

Ruins

Collecting memories like they're artifacts
If I keep enough, then maybe
I can build my heart back
Or at the very least remember
why we went wrong

Clarity

Maybe I'm not as ok as I want to believe
Maybe those broken pieces I keep denying
are attracting the wrong souls
Who linger way too long trying to take away
whatever light I have left, and I let them
Maybe it's time to fess up that it's not them, it's me

Eggshells

Your disappointment is like a hand over my mouth
Emotions caught up in my throat
I'm plugging myself up
Threading my way through the tension
You're all I have
I don't think I'll ever be enough for you
How silly of me to try

Imbalance

I just want to clear my mind
Just want it to not hurt
Holding back, I'm always holding back
Can't you see I'm breaking under the weight
of wanting to keep you happy?
I'm tired, exhausted
I don't even know what I want anymore
I stopped asking
I know people say things out of anger, but fuck
how many cuts are too many?

War Zone

I continue to fight a losing battle
Praying this tribulation will cease
Or at least that I will have the strength to sustain
Each day I wake and wonder
if this is really love
or am I just not brave enough to leave
Rapid-fire shots, words like venom
I yearn for the peace of mind from a smile
or the comfort of arms to cuddle in
The warmth in your eyes has faded
I'm not fighting anymore
Loving myself is already enough of an uphill battle

Devotion

May your heart never break
But if it should
I'll be here to pick up the pieces

May your soul never grow weary
But if it should
May the light of my soul rejuvenate yours

May your legs never give out from under you
But if they should
I will carry you wherever you need to go

May your hand never feel lonely
But if it should, my friend
know that my hand is always yours to hold

No Stars in Brooklyn

We have the past, the present
and we are the future
We are history's notes
and someone's dream comes to fruition
We are ambition, We are the Hustle, We Set the Bar
But, O, God, what I would give
to look up and see the stars
To be in awe of Your magnificence
Your celestial beauty painted
against the canvas of the sky
In that moment, I would know how small I am
My life lacking no significance
due to my size in the greater scheme of things
I'm a little light walking these streets
When my time has come to pass
and if I should be worthy of Your gates
Lord, please cast my Soul into the sky
and let someone look up, hoping to find me

Futile

Chased from room to room on delicate feet
Clusters of words try to fight through the sobs
Eyes once sweet and enticing
The brightest sort of welcome
Now look steely through mine, demanding silence
Hands tug hands
Pull and push
Anything to stop the departure

Crushed

I listened in utter shock and disbelief
The mouth that kissed me the night before
was now rapidly bringing me to tears
Not missing a beat as he ripped me apart
I kept telling myself through it all
that he loved me
Until I couldn't anymore

Reality Check

You were merely my creation
A testament to my inability to accept the truth
I ignored the bruises
In my mind, there was painted an amazing picture
of a man you never manifested to be
All that's left of you now are the scars on me

Prince Charming

I rushed to fill in the gaping holes
I didn't even notice the foundation was giving way
I built and rebuilt and fixed what I could
of our home
I was the only one fixing it
You watched, you criticized
and when it came down on me
You walked away
I don't know why I expected you to save me
I didn't care enough to save myself

The Shoe Don't Fit

It wasn't that the timing was wrong
It wasn't that I never could get the words out right
You were always a lesson wrapped in a disaster
I'm ok that you didn't turn out to be
My happily ever after

Misguided

Maybe I don't know what Love is
The only kind I cherish hurts
It whips like a storm through my life
Destroys everything in its path
Unearths my insecurities and fears
then just like that it's gone
Leaving me to rebuild and repair
No foundation, no substance
Just the better part of who I am scattered for miles

Selfish

My mile is your inch
My 80 percent, your 20
I love you with all I have
You love me with all you can give at the moment
My "I don't want you to leave"
Is your "I won't make you stay"
My "I'm at the edge of this"
Is your "I thought you were going to leave anyway"
My "I Love you"
Is your "I Love you, but I have dreams"
I guess we were both guilty of something

Trust Issues

She gave herself in small doses
so when people left it would hurt less
As relationships came and went
the doses became smaller
till she no longer felt the need to give

Thoughtless

You knew the whole time
You were just too much of a coward to say it
So, you pretended, you lied
even tried to fool yourself into believing
that this was something you wanted
All the while you waited
Pined over a love you dreamed of
versus the one you had
You thought nothing of the heart
you dragged to the door
when you left to be with someone else

Never Enough

Your name is engraved in my heart
and plastered onto the broken pieces of my mind
You use me, abuse me, and I come back every time
Fed by lies, I'm not sustaining
Love is blinding
All I ever wanted you to do was fight for me
Bandages on the wounds that never healed
Too worried about how you would feel
and if you would see weakness in my pain
and decide to leave

Lewis

I've seen forever in brown eyes
Tasted love's truth on full lips
I've stared at him so long he must think I'm crazy
If only he knew how long I've been searching
I'm tempted to ask, "What took so long?"
It doesn't even matter now, though
For I find joy in every minute, every second spent
with a man I've only dreamed of
whom I now get to dream with

Strain

Head pounding, soul weary
She's trying to think of a happy ending
But pen to paper won't fix this
Emotions spewed out won't make this better
Words have been beaten to death
Solutions have hung themselves

Salvation

We search within lost souls
and through the lies for the truth
The unwavering absolution
that someone saw us
for who we are and loved us

Discernment

These eyes have seen more pain and tribulation
than they knew they could bear
The things they wished
they would have shut themselves to
are the exact reasons they remain open
For if history is to be written
they refuse to let lies be told

Speechless

I remember nothing was quite as frightening
as the silence
The yelling I could stand
The harsh words revealed a truth
you normally were hesitant to speak
The silence, though
was riddled with a heavy uncertainty
I didn't know what to say then, still don't

Gwyneth

Back against the fridge
sliding down like the tears on my face
I knew it then; I knew for a while
The empty excuses
It's like you weren't even trying anymore
One foot out the door, the other in my throat
I knew I should leave; it's just the thought of it all
left me at a loss for words
Emptier than your attempts to avoid me
A friend picked me off the floor
You were never coming
I never belonged; I lost myself trying to

New Age Love

She chases you while you chase another
All chasing some profound feeling
that none of you are prepared enough to receive
let alone nurture
This is sad; nothing is like it used to be

Confirmation

If you want something different
you have to stop accepting what you're used to

Circles

We ignore the red flags, fall for the same lies
We see a bit of our past in our present
but convince ourselves it'll be different
We daydream that this time it'll turn out right
It all comes to a head
at the same place we've once been
Broken and confused
grasping at straws of rationalization
We love, we hurt, we lose
We forget to heal, to learn, to grow
We move forward
but we never really break the cycle

Admission

I'm trying to remember the person you were
before the arguments, the fights, and it all went bad
I just can't
It would be fooling myself into believing
you're someone that you're not anymore

Imperfect

Every trace was erased
Each text message, photo, every handwritten note
tossed in the trash with the other sentiments
Memories aren't that easy, though, or convenient
Just when you think you have it all together
One pops right in just to remind you
of how broken you really feel

Forgiveness

I will no longer mourn the inches of me
that loved you

Fuel

I don't want to just surpass the low standards
you think I deserve
I want to completely demolish
the thought that you had
that I was somehow less than
All based on your opinion alone
I am not angry; I'm determined
Thank you for the fuel, but the fire is all mine

Ceasefire

I think this is the quietest we've ever been
Is silence always this thick?
Or is the weight of our words lingering?
Why is it we don't hesitate before verbally
destroying the ones we claim to Love?
Slashing their dignity into pieces
then leaving them to repair it
I wanted to reach out and touch you
From the look on your face
you wanted to say something
anything to make this all right
But there was nothing
Forgiveness wouldn't be instant here
So, we just sat in our regrets
Each waiting for the other
to make the first move

The Fall

There was truth in our silence
Pain and anger in the tension
We fought to stay, fought to let go
Sometimes we just fought for the heck of it
I think we stopped knowing the difference
Then, eventually, we just stopped
Stopped talking
Stopped trying
Stopped caring
The only thing we didn't stop
was the other from leaving

Good Morning

I awake, my hair a mess
My limbs twisted and tangled with yours
I stop and listen to your heartbeat
thinking this is what it's all about
This is paradise
Loved devotedly, cherished deeply
and understood by this man
who will awake and kiss me
Despite my morning breath

Transparent

I like that we have our own language
It requires no words
One look and you know what I'm thinking
I hate and love that there's no hiding
who I am from you

Evolution

For too much of my life
I've apologized when I wasn't wrong
all to make a situation better
I'm not going to be that person anymore

Conformity

I feel where we fail
is that we yearn so deeply to be accepted
that we willingly give up the pieces
that make us different for fear of judgment

Trapped

Pining over loves lost
and fated to ask "what if?"
Somehow, we got lost in the past
Dooming ourselves to never forget

Life of a Poet

My past looks like ripped paper
and tattered notebooks
Love lost scrawled on Post-it notes
for former lovers who'll never read them

Therapy

I am thankful for all of the pieces of my heart
that got broken
It was therapeutic putting it all back together

Flatline

You're waiting for that little bit of hope
to have a lifeline
For all your patience and resilience to finally pay off
You're waiting for that person
to realize how good you are for them
Thing is, you can't force someone to see
what they don't want to

Settled

I let you mistreat me
It wasn't because I loved you
That was a lie I told both of us to justify staying
It was because I didn't love myself enough
to leave and go out and get better

Conditional Love

Here I was thinking I was good enough
When, in truth, you wanted me to be
a little less like me
and a bit more like the person
you pictured I could be
Funny how we love someone, flaws and all
Until the flaws start showing

Envy

The grass is always greener on the other side
When you stop watering your own

2A

My favorite color is green
I'm touching it as if it's on someone else's body
Remnants of last night are playing in my head
An accusation was made; there was yelling
It grew louder and louder
I put my hand in his face
The next moments were a haze
As if I were watching rather than living it
He punched a wall
I stood in his path
when he tried to walk away from me
He gathered my things and threw them into the hall
I clung to the foot of a table
as the next thing he tried to toss out was me
He screamed in my face, and then it stopped
Then came the silence
A clawing, all-encompassing quietness
I should have left
Yet here I am, lying beneath his arm, awake
The pain and green bruises
proof that it wasn't a nightmare
Sadly, green is still my favorite color

Adjusted Perception

There were always hints
Clues of what boiled beneath
You made them easy to ignore
Until the pain became more consistent
I never understood the women who stayed
I'm ashamed of my judgment, my ignorance
I used to say there must be something
missing in them
What is missing in me?

Regret

To say I miss you would be an understatement
To confess every waking moment
I'm thinking about you
Would be nothing short of the truth
I must apologize
because the very thing I took for granted
is what I yearn for most now, your presence
I desire your touch, your kiss
or even just to hear you
say those beautiful three words
I didn't appreciate everything we were
and now it's all I want

Sentry

To all the women lying in bed unable to sleep
because of ghosts of past relationships
or bad decisions haunting them at night
you are not alone
You go ahead and get some rest
I'll take the first shift

Drained

I hope your lips will kiss
the wounds that you've created
That you will have the answer to all my questions
Be a healing balm for the pain
I'm treating you as if you're something divine
You're barely a footnote in my story
You're a man who gives in to whims and impulses
Who needs someone to make you feel
like you're more than what you are
To call you a man does the integrity of the word
a great injustice
You're just a boy with low self-esteem
who needs to crush others to feel important
Still, you know what to say to keep me in place
Balanced between going and staying
When you're ready
you reel me in with the lies you know I need
I know what you're feeding me
It just hasn't felt as good lately
It's lacking some luster
Or maybe I'm just tired
I think I want to stop now
Whatever you were before, you aren't now

Sugarcoated

I lied to myself
Edited my thoughts so
you would seem like a better man
Censored my words so
our history wouldn't seem as bleak
Weighed no more with the burden
of trying to make it right
I can admit
no, you weren't a good boyfriend
and, yes, I always deserved better

Safe

Your eyes dance with a light
that captivates me to stare into your soul
Your spirit attracts me to the gates
of your heart to linger
The beat strikes a note that I respond
to with an increasing rhythm of my own
In that place, simple as it may be
I've found my home

Limbo

Some people are so stuck on who I was
that who I am never even had a chance

Standoff

Some would say I dodged a bullet
but the wounds I'm left with
would laugh in disdain
For what is a burning hole and bleeding flesh
compared with a broken heart and shattered faith

Spring Cleaning

I'm a hoarder of memories
Crammed between how beautiful my present is
and what my past has done to me
It's not monsters that I fear but the remnants of you
that I have left under my bed
The notes, the cards, the little trinkets
I decided to clear it all out today
It's easier to look back; you already know the ending
I think it's time I actually give myself a chance
to embrace the here and now

The Chase

Some people run
cause they want someone to chase them
I just don't have it in me anymore
to be the person who follows behind you
every time you decide to leave

Robbed

I've had a lot of people
who said they loved me
treat me like shit
I wonder which one of us
had the more fucked-up definition

Dedication

She went through a snowstorm
just to lie by his side
He wouldn't even walk through the rain

Exiled

I remember what you used to be like
I don't know who you are now
I wish I did
I hate the feeling that
I've been left out of your life

Stand Tall

There will be those who seek to destroy you
and everything you stand for
No matter what, keep building

Groove

It's not so much you
as it is the routine of loving you
that makes it hard to quit

Distress

What is it I'm afraid of, you ask?
It is simply of losing you
and in doing so
losing a far greater part of myself

Refuge

I escape with each stroke of my pen
Each emotion given life on this page
I'm free
No longer left to be crushed by my inability to let go
They stay, they always stay, and I let them
They follow me from room to room
relationship to relationship
Here, though, it's just me and the truth
Sometimes I don't want to leave
Just remain tucked safely in the black and white
I know once I depart
I'll fall somewhere in the gray
Using my emotions and inability to cope
as an excuse not to deal with the issues
For now, I'm just going to stay here
I'm not weak, just scared
that once I clean everything up
there won't be anything left

Warrior

She goes on
Despite the fears, struggles
obstacles and disappointments
She lives for Love of self
Love of life
And maybe one day
for the Love of someone else

Empty Garden

I've taken stock of my life
I've loved people who've hated me
Been loyal to a fault to those
who've disrespected me
Gone out of my way for people who
had no problem leaving me
Give, I always give
It's what I know how to do
I take so little in return
Normally left with only my delusions
of the devotion I surely must be sowing
There was no garden
No radiant, velvet blooms of adoration
Just a bare, grim reality
that I couldn't see past my own fantasies
There was nothing
I had grown nothing
Not even a bloom of love for myself

My Story

My words have followed me through the years
From adolescent love to the pains of womanhood
Stuffed within notebooks, in bins and book bags
Concealed within pockets of purses
Jotted-down notes in my cell phone
The passion, the agony, and ultimately
my awakening has been there
Always hinting, always reminding
This is who I've been, who I am

Just So You Know

You are a light
despite the darkness
that has tried to consume you

anywho, I love you.
　—r.h. Sin

Born to Love, Cursed to Feel Revised Edition
copyright © 2021 by Samantha King Holmes. All rights reserved.
Printed in the United States of America. No part of this book
may be used or reproduced in any manner whatsoever without written
permission except in the case of reprints in the context of reviews.

Andrews McMeel Publishing
a division of Andrews McMeel Universal
1130 Walnut Street, Kansas City, Missouri 64106

www.andrewsmcmeel.com

21 22 23 24 25 VEP 10 9 8 7 6 5 4 3 2 1

ISBN: 978-1-5248-6894-9

Library of Congress Control Number: 2021940436

Editor: Patty Rice
Art Director: Holly Swayne
Production Editor: Elizabeth A. Garcia
Production Manager: Cliff Koehler

ATTENTION: SCHOOLS AND BUSINESSES
Andrews McMeel books are available at quantity discounts with
bulk purchase for educational, business, or sales promotional use.
For information, please e-mail the Andrews McMeel Publishing
Special Sales Department: specialsales@amuniversal.com.